Katy PERRY

THE ULTIMATE POP PRINCESS

Mason Crest

Contents

[redacted]

Mason Crest
450 Parkway Drive, Suite D
Broomall, PA 19008
www.masoncrest.com

Printed and bound in the United States of America.

10 9 8 7 6 5 4 3 2

Cataloging-in-Publication Data on file with the Library of Congress.

ISBN: 978-1-4222-3248-4
ebook ISBN: 978-1-4222-8661-6

Written by: Michael Heatley

Images courtesy of PA Photos

Intro

Katy Perry arrived on the pop scene in 2008 when it was very much in need of a wake-up call. Five short years later she is a certified megastar and is being talked of as the new Madonna, a girl who has the entertainment world firmly at her feet.

But Katy is very much in touch with the internet generation, using social media to keep close to her fans. The past few years have brought many triumphs with eight Grammy nominations, a smash hit movie, and two platinum albums, not to mention hit singles, but also personal anguish. Her marriage to British actor Russell Brand hit the rocks within months, leading to a great deal of less-than-welcome media coverage. There's no doubt Katy's religious upbringing helped her keep her feet firmly planted on the ground.

Katy Perry is the only artist to spend over 52 consecutive weeks in the Top 10 of the Hot 100 and was named 2012 Woman of the Year by music-business magazine *Billboard*. The big question is whether she can, like Madonna, reinvent herself periodically and sustain a lifetime career. Can she become a brand (with no capital B), write songs for others, and take her own music in an evermore-fascinating direction? In short, will this Teenage Dream who became a California Gurl grow up and take her fans with her for the ride?

This fact-packed publication charts Katy's past, investigates her present, and speculates on her equally fascinating future.

Fact File

Full Name: Katheryn Elizabeth Hudson
Birthday: October 25, 1984
Place of birth: Santa Barbara, California, USA
Nationality: American
Star sign: Scorpio
Height: 5' 7"
Weight: 123 lbs (56 kg)
Vital statistics: 32C-26-33
Color of hair: Jet black (allegedly naturally blonde)
Color of eyes: Blue-grey
Religion: Christian
Educated: Dos Pueblos High School, Santa Barbara, Music Academy of the West
Family: Parents Keith and Mary Hudson, elder sister Angela, and younger brother David
Marital status: Divorced (married to Russell Brand 2010-12)
Nickname/internet alter ego: Kitty Purry
Distinguishing marks: "Jesus" tattoo on her left wrist
Favorite TV show: *SpongeBob SquarePants*
Favorite colors: Blue and pink
Favorite foods: Thai and Mexican food, spaghetti, crepes, ice cream
Favorite animal: Cat
Favorite fruit: Watermelon
Favorite song: *Killer Queen* by Queen
Favorite artists: Queen, the Beach Boys, Heart, Gwen Stefani, Rufus Wainwright, Imogen Heap, Madonna
Dream duet partner: Rihanna
Instrument played: Guitar
Sports and games: Golf, ice skating
Ambition: To launch her own record label

Katy Perry
PART OF ME
Katy Perry
PART OF ME

CHAPTER 1:

Early Years

Katheryn Elizabeth Hudson is a name you might not immediately recognize. But it will surely ring a few more bells when you realize she grew up to be singing superstar Katy Perry. She changed it because of the similarity to blonde movie star Kate Hudson; Perry was her mother's maiden name.

But you may still be unaware that Katy Hudson, as she was first known in professional circles, had a career in gospel music and even recorded an album in 2001 before turning to pop. That's hardly surprising since parents Keith and Mary were very much involved in Christian ministry. And that's where Katy's musical education began. She learned to sing in her parents' church, and did so until the age of 16.

Katy's arrival in the world on October 25, 1984 followed that of elder sister Angela; a brother, David, would complete the family unit. Yet the environment in which she lived was far from typical of a future pop star. "It was kind of an island," she said in an interview for *Blender* magazine in October 2008. "We spoke in tongues. We knew there was this one way, and all the other ways were wrong."

The world of arts, popular culture, and entertainment were barely known to her, and that made those early years far from easy. It wasn't that she lacked love and attention from her parents, but she was forbidden to do things most children take for granted. "I didn't have a childhood," she has said, revealing that her mother never read her any books except the Bible and that she wasn't allowed to eat "deviled eggs" or refer to the vacuum cleaner as a "Dirt Devil." She dutifully went to church on Sunday morning, Sunday evening, and Wednesday night.

A number of different forces were at work on the young Katy, a girl whose life was a collection of paradoxes. While her parents embraced the importance of beliefs over possessions, the area they lived in, Santa Barbara, is a very wealthy, well-to-do suburb of California. Her father Keith was also no ordinary minister, sporting an earring and diamante crosses and favoring leather trousers. Her mom, of Portuguese descent, apparently went on a date with late, great, guitar legend Jimi Hendrix back in the swinging Sixties. Little surprise, then, that there was soon a "bad girl/good girl" conflict going on in the mind of the child of two pastors.

The natural instinct of any teenager is to rebel – and, when growing up, Katy freely admits she "did a 180," came off the rails, and wasn't "a typical Christian." She has confessed to doing "lots of bad things" during her adolescence, and began drinking when she hit her teens. "I started spending Sunday mornings crying and hung over. Because crying is what you *do* when you're hung over. So my dad started telling me about when he was my age."

Her father, a bit of a rebel in his time, proved surprisingly understanding, so Katy is now very protective of her parents' beliefs even though she doesn't share them. "I don't try to change (my parents) any more, and I don't think they try to change me. We agree to disagree," she's said, adding: "I come from a very non-accepting family, but I'm very accepting."

In her autobiographical movie *Part Of Me*, screened in 2012, Katy recalled that when she was five she attended a

■ **LEFT: Katy with her parents Keith and Mary Hudson.**

■ RIGHT: Katy with members of her family.

revival meeting along with a few thousand people. The preacher came up to her and told her she would sing a hymn – and she did. But that was far from all. She found she had invented her own songs, "ditties that went round in my head," and she'd sing them in the shower or while she was walking along the road. Something out of the ordinary was definitely happening.

Both parents recognized their wayward daughter's talents, even if her behavior wasn't always what they hoped for. Her mother recently confirmed that she is proud of her daughter's success, telling *Vanity Fair* magazine that it was meant to be. "The Lord told us when I was pregnant with her that she would do this." In fact, it was Mary who first suggested her younger daughter took music lessons to develop her obvious talent.

Her understandably proud father also encouraged her to sing at every opportunity. "My dad would give me $10, which is a lot of money when you're nine, to sing at church, on tables at restaurants, at family functions, just about anywhere."

She'd started singing because "I was at that point in my childhood where I was copying my sister and everything she did." When Angela went out Katy would borrow the cassette tapes her sister sang along to and practice every song until she was word- and note-perfect – an early example of the perfectionist nature that has helped get her to the top of the pop tree.

Impressive as that was, copying Angela was still a long way from the revelation 13-year-old Katy underwent at a friend's

PART OF ME

house one day. "We're trying on all our outfits, like girls do, and out of nowhere I heard the lyrics to *Killer Queen*. Time stood still. The music was totally different from anything I'd heard. The heavens opened and saved me. From then on, Queen have been my biggest influence."

In high school, depending on where you stood, she was either mixing with the wrong crowd or already standing out from the crowd. Katy described herself as "a hop-around. I hung out with the rockabilly crew, the guys who were trying to be rappers, the funny kids."

Having been exposed to Freddie Mercury and company, she now wanted to know everything about pop and smuggled a Nirvana album into her house. Successful female singers Joan Jett and Pat Benatar were also early role models, while a series of summer camps she went to – one surf camp in particular – started to make her examine beliefs she had previously obeyed unquestioningly.

When she met a guy she liked, for instance, she asked herself questions about why she should "save herself" for marriage. "I was like, I don't know if I can hold that promise because this guy at camp is really cute," she later recalled. "Sex wasn't talked about in my home, but I was a very curious young girl."

Questions were asked when her mother discovered a thong in her underwear drawer, but the genie was out of the bottle. Katy Hudson was no longer walking around with her eyes closed; for better or for worse, she was a young woman with all the usual hopes, wishes, and desires that follow.

OF ME
can be
JULY 5
DIGITAL 3D

CHAPTER 2:
LA Woman

Music was turning out to be Katy's escape route from her sheltered life. And things got even better when she enrolled at the Music Academy of the West. This was in Montecito, a rich town near Santa Barbara, and among its many famous alumni was the legendary pop songwriter Burt Bacharach. She began playing acoustic guitar and singing, something she still sometimes does.

Katy's education now included all kinds of music, even Italian opera. She also attended swing-dancing classes – "My Forties education," she's since called it – learning the Lindy Hop and Jitterbug and picking up elements of her flamboyant image. She admits, though, that dancing has not come as naturally to her as singing. "I can't dance. Honestly. When I try the sweat is pouring off me. It's all an act."

But dancing ability or otherwise wasn't an issue to the musical talent scouts who spotted her potential after hearing her sing in church. This meant regular trips to the capital of country, Nashville, Tennessee, that certainly advanced her musical education. "When I was 14 or 15, I started recording gospel songs and be [sic] around amazing country music veterans and learn how to craft a song and play guitar."

The end result was an album, *Katy Hudson*, released by the Red Hill label in October 2001. This went all but unnoticed outside religious circles, but remains an impressive collection created by one so young. Katy had a hand in writing all 10 songs – five on her own, the others with assistance. Highlights included *Growing Pains*, with its musical nod to Queen, the jazzy *Last Call* and the Sara McLachlan-inspired *When There's Nothing Left*. The opening track *Trust In Me* was released as a single, to be followed by another, *Search Me*.

ABOVE: Katy's early solo work was compared with Alanis Morissette's work.

BELOW: Glen Ballard (left) pictured at the premiere of *Part of Me*.

The release was quite an achievement for a girl in her mid teens, with much emotional growing still to do. *Katy Hudson* received a favorable review from Russ Breimeier of *Christianity Today*, who called her "a remarkable young talent, a gifted songwriter in her own right who will almost certainly go far in this business." Her songwriting skills, he concluded, "are so strong, it's difficult to believe she's only 16 – and was merely 15 when she wrote most of these songs."

In a retrospective review, Stephen Thomas Erlewine from the *AllMusic* internet website, also complimented Katy's songwriting, comparing it to Canadian alt-rocker Alanis Morissette. He gave it a favorable three-star review, but commented with the clear benefit of hindsight that the album "is only instructive as the first act in a prefab pop star's career." As for the singer herself, "All those songs I wrote were very important to me at the time. I wrote about everything I knew then."

Katy supported the release by accompanying Phil Joel, former bassist for the Christian rock group Newsboys, on the Strangely Normal tour; other acts included LaRue, Luna Halo, Earthsuit, and V*Enna. On its first appearance the *Katy Hudson* album was a commercial failure, selling a small number of copies reckoned to be in the hundreds.

Production and distribution of the album ceased after Red Hill Records folded at the end of 2001. But that was not the end of the story. Perhaps predictably in the wake of her current popularity, it was re-released on iTunes on June 1, 2012.

One advantage of the label disappearing was that it helped Katy wipe the slate clean. Footage on YouTube of early Katy performances reveal that, although she's playing reverential Christian music, she had a real rapport with the audience, the occasional wisecrack hinting that there was a rebel inside Katy Hudson waiting to get out.

But pop fan Katy was finding it harder and harder to lead her double life. She still wasn't officially allowed to listen to what her mother called "secular music" or watch MTV. "I was becoming successful but it was really tough; the only music I was allowed to listen to was Christian music." But things were about to change as she took the decision to "go pop." "It took a little time for my parents to adjust when I stopped singing Gospel."

The next stage on the journey to stardom for the 17-year-old Katy Hudson was a relatively short one of 100 miles, heading south along the Californian coast road from Santa Barbara to Los Angeles. She hooked up with producer Glen Ballard after being impressed by Alanis Morissette, whose multi-platinum *Jagged Little Pill* album he produced. It had been the breakthrough album of 1995, its supercharged singer-songwriter sound, giving the Canadian singer six hit singles including the Grammy-nominated *Ironic* as well as a chart-topping album worldwide.

Katy had traveled to LA with her mother as chaperone, and turned on the previously forbidden VH1 music television at their hotel. As chance would have it, Ballard was being interviewed about his work with Morissette, and what he was saying struck an immediate chord. Katy expressed an interest in working with him, and the initial collaborator she'd traveled to meet was able to arrange an introduction. Ballard was impressed with the song Katy played with him, and, as she explains, "He called me the next day and said 'I want to move you to Los Angeles. I want to help fulfill your dreams.' He kinda looked out for me for three years."

So far, so good. But Katy was finding one major problem with making her name – someone else already had it! Every journalist would bring up Kate Hudson, the actress then enjoying screen success in *Almost Famous*, and it was not only becoming tiresome but was proving a barrier to her progress. Katy, then 20, was "wiser than her years," said one journalist who met her, and she certainly made a wise decision. As soon as she changed her name the real Katy Perry was born.

In 2004 Katy joined forces with Lauren Christy, Scott Spock, and Graham Edwards, three songwriters and producers known as The Matrix. The Matrix

shine

had been one of the hottest production teams of the last decade, working with the likes of Christina Aguilera, Avril Lavigne, Backstreet Boys, Hilary Duff, and Ronan Keating, but they were no longer top of the tree and clearly thought adding Katy's talents was the perfect idea to revive their fortunes.

For one reason or another it didn't work out that way but in 2009, after the success of Katy's debut solo album *One Of The Boys*, The Matrix decided to release the album they'd recorded with her on their own record label, Let's Hear It Records. Lauren Christy denied it was a cash-in release, saying "We're not releasing it on a major label, and it's not called *Katy Perry And The Matrix*."

The intended single from the album, *Broken*, saw Katy share the spotlight with British singer Adam Longlands on a pop tune that sounds like an Avril Lavigne track. Among the other Perry-fronted songs on the album are the new-wavy *Take A Walk*, ballad *You Miss Me*, string-laden *Just A Song*, and *Would You Care*, a song about self-obsessed pop stars. It's worth hearing for any fan curious about Katy's "wilderness years."

Away from this project, Katy had recorded some songs with Glen Ballard that led to her briefly being labeled "The Next Big Thing" by *Blender* magazine. But this endorsement was to prove something of a false dawn, as the teenager was still to suffer a series of disappointments as she sought to make an impression on the wider world.

She recorded an album's worth of material with Ballard, but the Island Def Jam label to which she was signed surprisingly rejected

ABOVE: Music executive Jason Flom played a crucial part in Katy's career.

the results. The fact she wasn't prepared to conform to people's expectations didn't help; Katy was never going to settle for being a carbon copy. "Kelly Clarkson and Avril Lavigne was what was really popular," she later remarked, "and people were always really scared to let me be me."

Undeterred, she signed to Columbia Records in 2004, but when another album was turned down she could have been forgiven for giving up. Although her career was still failing to take off, some of the songs she'd written like *I Do Not Hook Up* were re-recorded by Kelly Clarkson, while the song *Simple* featured on the soundtrack of a movie, *The Sisterhood Of The Travelling Pants*. The record they came from, which was due to come out in 2005, was circulated to the press and made her a known quantity, even though it was never officially released. Some of the songs made it onto her first pop album.

The years before Katy found fame found her struggling to stay afloat financially – in fact, at the point when she signed with current record label Capitol, she was two months behind on her car payments, couldn't pay her rent, and was about to move back in with her parents. She had been reduced to shopping for outfits in her friends' closets and looking for free samples of mascara. "I was completely broke," the now megastar recalls. "I used to borrow outfits, get my makeup done at makeup counters, and then sneak into events."

Few artists who have reached 24 and found themselves without a record label three times carry on and make it. But the same determination that got her Glen

Ballard as producer served Katy well. It was a low point in her career, with all the negative feedback, but she refused to give up. She was persistent and kept faith in her own ability. So when she met up with record-company executive Jason Flom she had high hopes. It took six months for him to call back, but his record label, Capitol Music Group, finally agreed to sign her in the spring of 2007.

She also lucked out when, making an appearance in the video for Gym Class Heroes' *Cupid's Chokehold* as the love interest of lead singer Travis McCoy, life imitated art. The single soared to the top of the charts and their love affair grew wings too – they would enjoy an on-off relationship until the end of 2008. At this point, Katy was adding to her live experience by opening for acts like Mika and the Starting Line.

She entered the studio yet again and this time emerged with a song that would, in November 2007, reach the public ear. Not that *Ur So Gay*, a song written about a real or imaginary boyfriend who started wearing her jeans and using her eyeliner, was going to make her a fortune, being initially offered as a free download on her MySpace page. What it *did* do was cause controversy, and bring inquisitive newspaper reporters flocking to her door.

"I was talking about an ex-boyfriend," she insisted, adding "it's not a negative connotation... the fact of the matter is that this boy *should've* been gay." Ironically her unique retro sense of style – as she put it, walking "a fine line between being a slut and being classy" – was winning her a significant gay fan following.

ABOVE: **Influential US blogger Perez Hilton.**

LEFT: **Katy pictured with then boyfriend Travis McCoy.**

Katy was at pains to explain the song was essentially a novelty and "wasn't meant to be a big single or show what the album is going to be all about. That was for my internet bloggers." Even the video was played for laughs, the characters being played by dolls against a roughly drawn backdrop.

One of those bloggers was Perez Hilton, the influential pop

gossip columnist who's made many a discovery. He was impressed enough to put it on his website... and no less a superstar than Madonna reacted to it. She went on record saying she was a fan – an endorsement a visually minded artist and pop singer like Katy could only have dreamed of. Madonna's lyrics, with their themes of female empowerment and honesty, had had a big impact on Katy's work, while her ability to reinvent herself would prove another shared trait.

Madonna first spoke about the song on the Phoenix, Arizona radio station KZZP-KRQQ where she prompted the hosts of the *John Jay and Rich Show* to "check it out on iTunes." Then on LA's KIIS-FM, she called the song "hilarious" and told DJ Ryan Seacrest he "*had* to hear it." The result was instant, and when the video for the song appeared on MySpace it clocked up one million views within a week.

Katy later recalled her incredulous reaction to the news she had a famous fan. "I was, like, *Madonna*? This is a *joke*! She's amazing, and she's someone I aspire to be like. That woman has stayed so consistent, and even like Gwen Stefani... they are consistent, ever changing, and appreciate their fans. They want to entertain people."

Successful as that first recording had been, it was the second (and her first physically released) single *I Kissed A Girl* that would propel Katy Perry to fame and fortune when it raced up the *Billboard* Hot 100 chart all the way to No. 1. After so many disappointments and false starts, Katy Perry, the former Katy Hudson, was well and truly on her way at last.

CHAPTER 3:

Breakthrough

When *I Kissed A Girl* was released in April 2008, it took the girl with blue hair, watermelon fetish, and kooky fashion sense – not to mention amazing musical talent – into the living rooms of millions of fans worldwide. By shooting to the top of the transatlantic charts, it established her as the sound and look teenage girls most wanted to copy. As for those risqué lyrics, well they didn't do sales any harm, either... and the song received a new lease of life when it was used in an episode of teen TV drama series *Gossip Girl*.

So what, or who, exactly inspired *I Kissed A Girl*? Katy, who understands the value of keeping gossip going, has never definitively said – but it could have been a crush on a 15-year-old classmate. Others have suggested it was the feelings stirred in her by glamorous movie actress Scarlet Johansson. But what does it really matter? The formula was very clever: in one critic's words, "It's not very

■ RIGHT: Dr. Luke.

sexual, but it's *naughty*," while another added "it's going to interest people but not cause a scandal." It's been suggested the song is a funny version of Alanis Morissette's breakthrough hit *You Oughta Know*... but with its title in Twitterspeak.

One thing was for sure – Katy had needed a big pop record to make sure she didn't slide back down the pop pole, and now she had one. Jason Flom, the man who signed her, thought her collection of songs was "very strong but lacking an undeniable smash or two that would work both at US pop radio and internationally." For that reason the label put her together with Dr. Luke (real name Lukasz Gottwald), now an established pop producer but then very much in the up-and-coming bracket.

The teaming proved an inspired one: the pair hit it off musically straight away and Katy had found someone who could help make her pop dreams a reality. Amazingly, they recorded *I Kissed A Girl* right at the end of the sessions when all the other material had been successfully cut – what might have happened had she not had that one song left in her locker?

Dr. Luke had his finger on the pulse of the pop world, having previously worked with such names as Ke$ha, Miley Cyrus, and Kelly Clarkson. Working with him would help Katy rival and then surpass those females, using her hit as the springboard to success.

Katy Perry had made a big pop record – now she needed it to be heard. So she toured the United States' radio stations day after day, talking to DJs and "pushing the product." The result was that it became the summer hit of 2008, shooting to No. 1 on the *Billboard* Hot 100 where it stayed put for seven straight weeks and tied with The Beatles as the Capitol Records act with most weeks at No. 1.

I Kissed A Girl had caught people's attention, but opinions differed as to whether it was pro or anti gay in its sentiments. As Katy herself explained, the song could even be seen as an innocent slumber-party anthem. "When we're young, we're very touchy-feely. We have slumber-party singalongs, we make up dance routines in our pajamas. We're a lot more intimate in a friendship than guys can be. It's not perverse but just sweet..."

What was certain was that it was a bit of fun and it connected with enough people to make it not only the pop song of the year but the 10th biggest digital single of the 21st century. It also inspired many a parody by the likes of "Weird Al" Yankovic, who mixed it with Lady Gaga's *Poker Face* to create a *Polka Medley*. TV series *Glee* was, needless to say, rather more respectful.

But the song that defined her was not something her parents were happy with. That said, mom Mary was there at almost every other gig, proving she had pride in her daughter if not necessarily in every word of the music she was producing. Mrs. Hudson

was quoted as saying her daughter's music was "shameful and disgusting," though Katy later told MTV that her mother was misquoted.

With all the hype and publicity surrounding Katy, her new album *One Of The Boys* just couldn't come soon enough for her army of new fans. Most, of course, thought it was actually her first, but its release in June 2008 saw it hit No. 9 in the US, 11 in Britain, and top the chart in Australia, Austria, Canada, Germany, Holland, Ireland, New Zealand, and Switzerland. Katy Perry was now on the music map.

A second song Katy had cut with Dr. Luke, *Hot N Cold*, stood out with its breathless pace and unforgettable "earworm" chorus, while other highlights included the tongue-in-cheek *If You Can Afford Me*, male-baiting *Mannequin*, and the closing *Fingerprints*. The singles *I Kissed A Girl* and *Ur So Gay* were present and correct, while *Waking Up In Vegas* certainly had future singles potential.

But it wasn't all bubblegum pop: as one critic put it, "*Lost* and *I'm Still Breathing* demonstrate her capacity to vary the emotional palette and pace without losing our attention." The Pink-influenced *Self Inflicted* was sad, yet upbeat and very powerful – one for fans to sing along to proudly – while Katy revealed "I get a lot of girls who come up to me and say, 'When I heard *Thinking Of You*, I felt that way to a T, but I never knew anyone who could put my feelings into words.'"

Singles success was still the top priority, though, and *Hot N Cold* was selected as the next to be taken from the album. It emerged in September and reached No. 3 in the Hot 100, as well as topping the charts in Germany, Canada, and Denmark. Its cute cover artwork had Katy speaking into a "watermelon phone," highlighting her unique sense of style.

It also caused one of the sillier controversies in Katy's – or any pop star's – career. She duetted on a child-friendly version of the new single with *Sesame Street*'s Elmo but, after the clip was previewed on YouTube, the guardians of decency weighed in and had it banned from the nation's TV screens. Katy's "crime" was wearing a top that was too low-cut...

It was all a long way from the image she'd been projecting on the Warped Tour, a traveling rock circus she'd joined three days after her debut album had been released. She followed in the footsteps of an early role model Gwen Stefani, who had played the tour back in 2000 with No Doubt, while female-fronted rockers Paramore had headlined the 2007 tour with lead singer Hayley Williams the standout performer of the entire festival line-up.

But our girl was clearly ready and willing to meet the challenge and measure up to her predecessors. "Warped is going to be grueling and hot, but I'm ready to survive it – even without showers," Katy said. "When Gwen did the tour she looked fabulous hopping around on stage in her little polka-dotted dresses. I'm so channeling that." Though she wasn't headlining, the crowd that gathered to see her 30-minute set was just as big as those watching bigger acts such as Angels & Airwaves, Motion City Soundtrack, and The Academy Is...

The idea of being a rock chick with a guitar, hiding behind black sunglasses, gave Katy cool credibility. But it wouldn't be long before she was trading those shades for the crown of queen of pop. And with that would come the development of her very own style.

She's explained it as similar to suffering from "multi-personality disorder – in a very good way, of course – when it comes to my fashion choices. When I first started playing around with my look, it was more of a Dita Von Teese pin-up thing."

Katy's kooky dress sense was proving as memorable as her music. She defined her fashion as "a bit of a concoction of different things. I really like to look like a history book. I can look Forties, I can look Fifties, hippie-chic, or sometimes I'll pull that Eighties Brooklyn hip-hop kid with the door-knocker earrings." And

Freddie Mercury was still a role model, not so much fashion-wise but in attitude. Said Katy: "He was flamboyant with a twist of the operatic, but – more importantly – he just didn't give a ****."

With a tour already booked and paid for, Katy's first gigs in Britain were to students even though she was already mega-successful in the States. British critics likened her to the five Spice Girls rolled into one. Journalists found her very approachable, one saying "she won't shoo you away, she'll look you in the eye and answer any question you throw at her – she's very open."

Unfortunately this outspoken honesty got her into hot water with homegrown heroine Lily Allen when Katy unwisely described herself as a "skinny version of Lily Allen." The slightly fuller-figured but equally feisty Miss Allen riposted that "I hear you are the answer to me," throwing a description on a record-company biography straight back in her face. Happily the two girls settled their differences without a catfight.

In February 2009, both *I Kissed A Girl* and *Hot N Cold* were certified three-times platinum by Recording Industry Association of America for their individual digital sales of over three million. A year later, the *Guinness Book of World Records* would recognize Katy as having achieved the "Best Start on the US Digital Chart by a Female Artist," having seen those first two singles sell over two million digital copies.

Next up on the singles front was *Thinking Of You*, released in January 2009 and one of three songs on the *One Of The Boys* album that Perry wrote all by herself. It was relatively disappointing in chart terms, only

■ **ABOVE: Katy performs on the Warped Tour.**

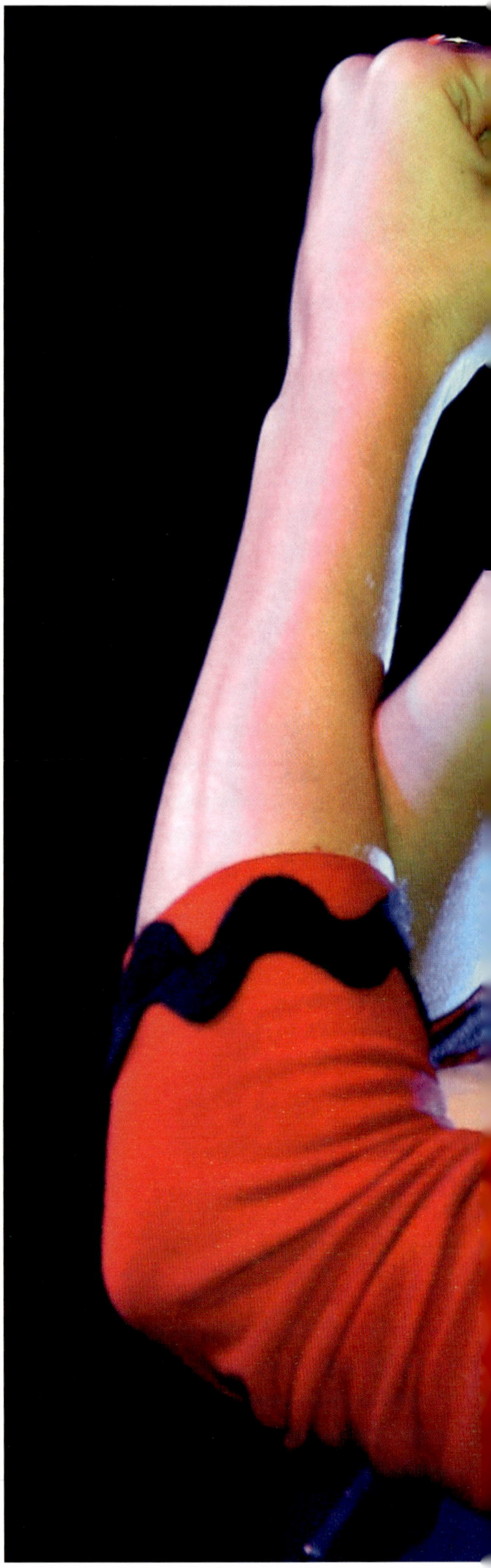

just making it into the Top 30. But any jealous whispers that Katy was on the slide were silenced once and for all when *Waking Up In Vegas* gave her another Top 10 entry three months later.

This final single from the album was inspired by Katy's own "fake

wedding" to a former boyfriend at age 21. "We went to Vegas on a whim and we decided to get fake married. We took all the pictures with the minister, with the fake cake, in the fake chapel, and got a fake marriage certificate." She was so proud of pulling off the stunt that she held on to the wedding dress and fake "marriage certificate" for three years.

"We went and bought a wedding dress and a suit at a thrift store, and scanned the pictures and the certificate to my family members, my manager at the time (and) totally freaked the s**t out of them. It was the most hilarious, stupid prank I've ever pulled."

Katy's profile was now truly international; *I Kissed A Girl* had topped the chart in nine countries as far apart as Australia and Austria. She was voted Best New Act at the 2008 MTV Europe Music Awards and would win Best International Female Artist at the 2009 BRITs. Back home, she was nominated for Best Female Pop Vocal Performance at the 2009 Grammy Awards, the first of eight nominations she's so far secured.

With all this media attention, she was being talked of as the new Madonna. Her flirtatious, cheeky, and naughty image

entertained her fans, and inspired her audience to dress up too. But the girl who had the entertainment world at her feet keep her feet firmly on the ground. Her religious upbringing remains important, and the Jesus tattoo on her left wrist is a reminder of where she comes from.

BELOW: Lily Allen, Dita Von Teese, Katy Perry, and Emma Watson attending the Christian Dior Spring Summer 2009 Ready-to-Wear Collection Show in Paris.

CHAPTER 4:

Hits and Splits

Successful as she'd been, Katy was still very much a rising star. She'd been so busy, in fact, that her life seemed all work, work, work. But her personal life had been notably less successful. The break-up with Travis McCoy at the end of the Warped Tour in which they'd both starred was an

acrimonious one, and prompted her to write the song *Circle The Drain* (which would be released on the *Teenage Dream* album) to tell the whole sad story.

Katy had dated notorious bad boy McCoy on and off throughout 2008, breaking up shortly after New Year

BELOW: Katy with Travis McCoy.

2009. The major problem had been McCoy's substance abuse, which he admitted to on his blog, Traviesblog.com. He wrote that he had been addicted to pharmaceuticals since the age of 15, and he would eventually check into rehab to confront his problem.

Having escaped lightly, some would say, Katy then got involved with Russell Brand, a self-confessed former drug addict and all-round excessive character. Long-time observers saw a parallel with Madonna's marriage

■ **ABOVE:** **Bad boy Russell Brand.**

to the actor Sean Penn in the late Eighties, which had been short, tempestuous, and headline-making. Curiously, according to Katy, her parents approved of the match. "My mother's in love with him. And my father, I think he sees a lot of himself in him."

Katy met her future husband on the set of *Get Him To The Greek*, a movie in which she had been offered a role. "My scene called for me to make out with him," she later recalled. "And on the way down the stairs after the scene, I was hopping like a bunny. I hop like a bunny when I'm happy – I get a bit childlike..." But with Katy still involved with Travis McCoy, she wasn't free to take things further. Ironically the scene was cut from the final movie, but Katy was amused rather than annoyed at that outcome.

Sparks flew when Katy and Russell met again in September 2009 at the MTV Video Awards, with Katy now unattached. When two strong personalities met sparks were always going to fly. But the attraction was that, as one eyewitness put it, neither party intimidated the other. "Russell made fun of her and she threw a can of juice at him!" It was the beginning of a major-league love affair, and anyone who saw Russell and Katy talking in their own little bubble long after their entourages had departed would have been left in no doubt that something was happening.

Russell popped the question around New Year's Eve while the pair were enjoying some rest and relaxation at a tiger sanctuary in India, and they announced their engagement to the world just three months later. "I'm excited to find a partner who can just be my team-mate," she gushed of a man whose addictive personality had, in the past, led the press to dub him a "serial love cheat." He was the archetypal bad boy, but, as with Travis McCoy, Katy was not to be dissuaded.

The happy couple returned to India in 2010, where they tied the knot on October 23. Big sister Angela was Katy's maid of honor. Everyone was wearing traditional Indian garb, there were ethnic folk musicians, while elephants and tigers were to be seen everywhere. It was not exactly the traditional American white wedding that Katy might have imagined, but it was outside her comfort zone and therefore pretty exciting. Spectacular, spiritual... it had the lot. And the blushing bride brought over a member of her family's American church to

■ LEFT: BFFs Katy and Rihanna.

conduct the service and redress the cultural balance.

Katy told *Harper's Bazaar* magazine that Russell's spiritual quest for sobriety, that included friendship with a guru, Radhanath Swami, made him more acceptable. "I always knew I wanted a great man of God, someone who was going to be an inspiration for people and also be a lovely husband and father," she says. "We're at different places in our lives, but we can still grow together. He's thought-provoking, articulate, a real advocate. I also definitely wanted to have a laugh. I have all that in him."

Katy and Russell, described by one critic as "both crazy outside personalities, almost like two cartoons come to life," were constantly in the public eye during the course of their brief marriage. The pair had two homes, a love nest in New York and a Hollywood-style estate near Los Angeles' Griffith Park, where Katy turned their three-car garage into a huge pink-painted dressing room in which she entertained her friends.

They both undoubtedly ended up with raised profiles in each other's countries – Russell was now being offered parts in big-budget Hollywood movies – but the pressures must have been immense.

And when Mr. and Mrs. Brand did meet the press, their differences seemed profound. Russell was the archetypal Brit who loved soccer, while Katy loved the California lifestyle she'd enjoyed since childhood and had no plans to quit her home state, let alone the United States in general. Partying was an issue, as apparently was the fact that Katy felt she was too young to settle down and produce children. On another note, Russell apparently didn't like Katy's closeness to fellow singer Rihanna, whom he considered a bad influence.

For her part, Katy didn't think being half of a couple would have an impact on her music. "I won't only be singing songs about being a married woman," she explained, elaborating that if Beyoncé could perform *Single Ladies* when everyone knew she was with Jay-Z then she, Katy, could pretend to be exactly who she wanted to be.

She certainly seemed happy to face the challenges before her. "I think you can have it all," she mused. "You just have to work really hard, because great things don't come easily. Everyone's been told that marriage is hard work, and it is: You have to make time for the things you love."

As for the possibility of producing little Perry-Brands at some future point, she was, on the face of it, happy with that too. "I want to have kids! I'm totally fine with saying that. I think some people are worried it's going to ruin their career, but I want to live a full life." Of course these were soundbites that could be (and were) revisited by the press when times were not quite so happy.

Sadly, less than a year later, Katy and Russell's marriage slowly imploded amid tabloid headlines. A planned vacation together turned into separate vacations, wedding rings vanished from fingers, and respective Twitter accounts were unfollowed in what became a painful and very public separation.

The fact that cultural differences split the couple was finally confirmed in December 2011, 14 months after the

■ RIGHT: With Aerosmith's Joe Perry (no relation) at the 2009 VMAs.

wedding. Russell was first to file for divorce citing "irreconcilable differences." As he later put it, "I think if you're someone who's really into mountain biking, it would be good to go out with someone who's into mountain biking, and if you're really into Eastern mysticism, go out with someone else who's into Eastern mysticism..."

Katy wouldn't speak publicly about the break-up, but an earlier interview had spelled out her views on what made a relationship work. "I think for me it's nothing about the big things; it's all about the little things, the details. You don't have to do big things that cost lots of money – all you have to do is call us back, tell us 'You're beautiful, I love you.' Send flowers when it's not our birthday..."

She might also have added "Don't take photos of us in bed without permission"... and had certainly been far from happy when Russell sent an unflattering photo of her makeup-less early-morning face to the many followers of his Twitter account. It was quickly deleted, and their marriage disappeared just as quickly not so long afterward.

Little had happened in Katy's life on the musical front since *One Of The Boys*, but in November 2009, shortly after the MTV Video Awards, she released an *Unplugged* album recorded for the television channel. It was also a DVD and contained a rare cover version, Fountains of Wayne's *Hackensack*, which she described as "a perfect pop ballad that really hits home." Other selections included *I Kissed A Girl*, *Ur So Gay*, *Thinking Of You*, *Lost*, *Waking Up In Vegas*, and a brand new original track, *Brick By Brick*.

In the words of one reviewer,

■ **BELOW:** **Katy pictured with Perez Hilton.**

"These selections highlight the full range and power of Perry's voice as she performs vocal acrobatics that, although somewhat superfluous, give new life to the existing lyrics." It was certainly true that the lyrics were clearer and more understandable in this format.

The performance was also surprisingly laid-back, as an internet blogger reflected. "Katy seemed a little self-conscious; her body language seemed more withdrawn than usual, she would lift her eyes to meet those of someone in the public then would quickly avert her gaze, and even her jokes were delivered in a soft voice. This was a refreshing surprise." The album was far from a big seller, peaking at No. 168 in the chart, but had shown fans another, more vulnerable side of their idol.

So far, so good for Katy Perry – *Unplugged* was an interesting diversion, but it was clear that Katy's next step would be crucial. The foundations had been laid for megastardom, but the wrong move could see her cast as a one-album-wonder.

In musical terms she herself had no doubts what she wanted to do and where she wanted to be. "In this past year and a half," she said, "I think some people have an idea of who I am or a little piece of the cake. I am really excited to be ever evolving and changing with my look, my music. It keeps me entertained as well. The next record will be very pop."

True to her word, she came up with the ultimate teen-friendly summer album – and the secret was she was working with Dr. Luke again. As they planned their collaboration she gave the man who helped her make her

breakthrough single a mix tape packed with frothy pop music from the likes of Abba and the Cardigans. The result, she hoped, would be "a summer record – it's roller-skating Nineties, it's Ace of Base, it's Cyndi Lauper, it's *more*..."

There had been pressure from the record company to come up with a lead single that was as catchy and quirky and as much fun as *I Kissed A Girl* – in short, a true feel-good anthem. And Katy delivered the goods and more with *California Gurls*.

She previewed the record at blogger Perez Hilton's birthday party, riding in on top of an elephant and dressed in a circus outfit. The yet-to-be-released single hit the DJ's decks, and there was not a guitar to be heard. This was a total pop record, without a shadow of a doubt. And it would cause her to become far showier in her stage act.

"I'm doing some dance now," she'd comment, "because the music has changed from the rock to a lot more of the pop, and I don't want to look like my mother on stage... I'm just trying to get my swagger back." Queen's theatrics and flamboyance that had so inspired Katy in her not-so-distant teenage years were finally making a comeback.

The release in August 2010 of second "mainstream" album *Teenage Dream* was not only notable for the quality of the music but the outrageous image of Ms. Perry lying naked on clouds of cotton candy. Clearly being banned from the *Sesame Street* airwaves had not discouraged her from showing off her "assets." As one commentator put it, "She has curves and she's not afraid to show them off. But she never dresses in a way that's vulgar – she dresses like a cartoon character or a doll. And men enjoy it too!"

Katy was clearly as excited as her fans about the new album. "It's a summer record," she beamed. "It's what I said I wanted earlier. I finally got it. We nailed it. There might be some really cool guest appearances. Some rappers from the West Coast, since I am a California girl."

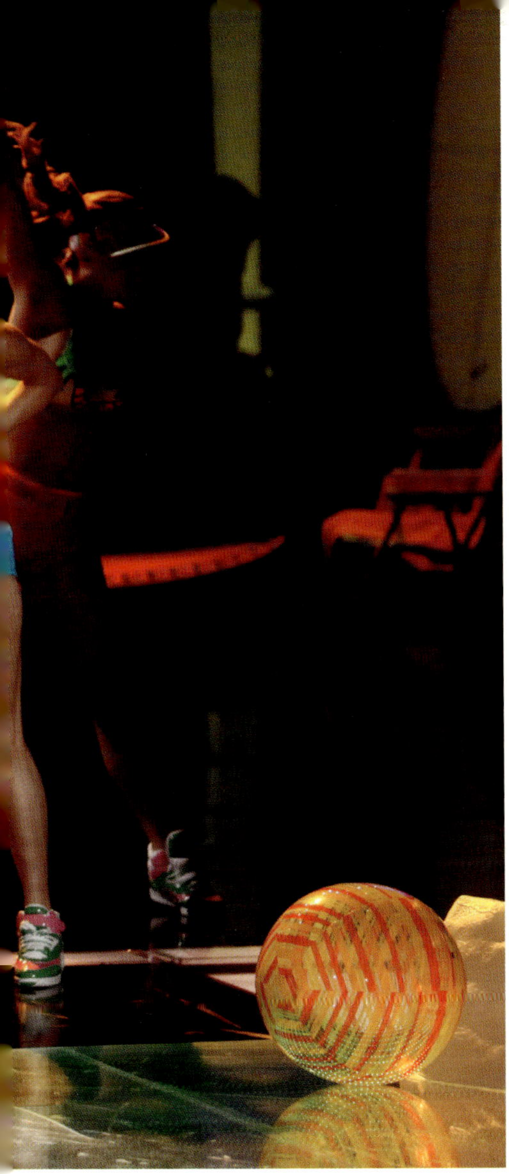

■ **LEFT: Katy Perry and Snoop Dogg perform at the MTV Movie Awards.**

True to her word, rapper Snoop Dogg showed his approval with a guest appearance and collaborations like this helped her to be taken seriously.

The result was the fastest rising Capitol Records album since country singer Bobbie Gentry's *Ode To Billie Joe* in 1967. *Teenage Dream* was five times platinum – a rags-to-riches American Dream. Katy was now technically in her twenties, but she certainly had mega teen appeal.

The US No. 1 success of *Teenage Dream* was just the beginning, as the album's catchy melodies, catchy lyrics, and singalong choruses brought hit after hit. With five US chart-toppers on board, this was a "Greatest Hits" in all but name. But critics quickly latched on to the cheeky *Peacock*, whose chorus guaranteed it would *not* be getting radio airplay any time soon!

The previously mentioned, achingly personal *Circle The Drain* was the odd song out on a feel-good album, while *The One That Got Away* was very thought provoking. Other highlights included *Heartbeat* and the closing *Not Like The Movies*, while she described *Who Am I Living For?* as "a song on my new record which talks about my convictions" and described her "own personal pilgrimage."

Teenage Dream's title track and *Firework* both made No. 1 and had pundits wondering exactly how far Katy could go. The success of *E.T.* and *Last Friday Night (T.G.I.F.)* made her the first female ever to have five No. 1 singles from one album, putting Ms. Perry firmly in the Michael Jackson bracket as far as sales success went.

More provocative and less cute than *One Of The Boys*, *Teenage Dream* was a perfect snapshot of Katy Perry, a self-styled "young woman, with my perspectives, convictions, anthems, and mottos. It's full of different dimensions. It has songs like *California Gurls* that are really fun and obvious, and then there are songs like *Firework* that would hopefully motivate you and make you want to move – and there are songs like *Not Like The Movies*, which is a love song. If you want to know about me, it's definitely the CD to get."

News came in November 2011 that seemed likely to change the course of Katy's career. Sony Music signed Dr. Luke to an exclusive five-year contract, meaning that the producer would no longer be able to create music for non-Sony acts. Luke was the mastermind behind the formula that has worked time and again for Katy, having produced *California Gurls*, *E.T.*, *The One That Got Away*, *Teenage Dream*, and of course the previous album's *Hot N Cold* and *I Kissed A Girl*.

There was also the chance that, with Luke now signing acts to his very own label, Katy might find herself competing with girls using the same sound that had brought her fame and fortune. She would have to come up with something that would keep her at least one step ahead of the competition.

CHAPTER 5:
Screen Dreams

Katy's next musical move was certainly eagerly awaited. But as she embarked on a sustained period of world touring – the California Dreams tour of 2011-12, which grossed a cool $60 million – Katy was on top of the pop world. And she found the challenge both mentally

ABOVE: A guest appearance as a judge on *American Idol*, with Simon Cowell and Kara DioGuardi.

and physically stimulating. "My concerts are an hour long, so I usually jump rope for half an hour beforehand to get warmed up. It's intense." She also had to share the tour bus with "14 sweaty men," but gave as good as she got in the on-the-road banter.

In-between tours she found time to pass on her wisdom as guest judge on TV's *American Idol*. It was reported in 2012 that she received a $20 million offer to be one of the series' new judges but turned it down due to a busy schedule – an indication of how fast her career had taken off. She'd also jetted into Dublin, Ireland, on a one-woman mentoring mission as a special guest of the UK franchise of *The X Factor*.

Appearing on the British TV talent show not only gave her publicity but also left them with her seal of approval. Katy, who wore a silver and turquoise mini-dress and purple stilettos, took to Twitter before making her judging debut to express her excitement, tweeting: "X FACTOR DUBLIN!!! Can't wait to spot a star!!!"

She had been one of the first generation of showbiz personalities to use the social media of Facebook and Twitter to keep in touch with fans. She used them to give her followers sneak previews and other favors, while she also had a bit of fun with alter ego Kitty Purry, her pet feline. Few stars are bigger users of social media than Katy; only Justin Bieber and Lady Gaga can rival her. The close link this gives her with fans is clearly something she treasures.

Videos had also played a big part in Katy Perry's successful career, and it was obvious that she was a natural for the big screen. Her first step to Hollywood stardom was a guest appearance (as the voice of the character Smurfette) in 2011's *The Smurfs*. "Smurfette was really just so fun to do! It's something that I really wanted to do and be a part of. I love watching those (children's) movies, whether it's *Up* or *Toy Story* and feeling good inside but also feeling really entertained or laughing out loud." But that was only the first step. She was about to tell her fans exactly where she'd come from.

■ **BELOW:** **With fans outside *The X Factor* auditions in Dublin, Ireland for the UK franchise.**

She had had an idea for an autobiographical movie for a while, and had sold it to Paramount studios. "*Part Of Me*," she said, was about "overcoming obstacles… a lot of it is about people wanting me to fit into an idea. But I wanted to create my own idea. Hopefully people will see that we are all going through a lot of the same things."

Certainly, the trials and tribulations she'd had to overcome had made for a story that would open the eyes of anyone thinking she was a

"manufactured," here today, gone tomorrow, pop star. On the other hand, she was adamant she wasn't setting herself up as someone whose example was to be followed. "If people want a role model," she laughs, "they can have Miley Cyrus!"

Katy was so convinced her idea was a hit that she put no less than $2 million of her own money into filming a movie that cost $12 million to make. "I knew I was either going bankrupt or about to have the biggest success of my life," she later explained, "but when I and they got really excited, I didn't know it was going to turn into such a big thing." There was never any doubt Katy and her backers would more than recoup her investment.

It mixed autobiography with recent concert footage from the California Dreams tour, recorded in November 2011 at Staples Center, Los Angeles. Katy told MTV news that "It's closing the chapter on *Teenage Dream*, but it's giving you such an inside perspective… This movie, you're going to see it from my best friend/buddy perspective – you're going to see exactly what I mean and feel and think about everything."

A major selling point was that it was shot in 3D, and glasses were designed for distribution in movie theaters that featured a white and red candy stripe motif in Katy's style. It was launched in the summer of 2012 with not one but two premieres, in Los Angeles on June 26 and in London on July 3. Needless to say Katy attended both.

BELOW: **Rumors of romance with American singer John Mayer.**

Concert footage was surprisingly sparse, though *Firework*, *California Gurls*, *Part Of Me*, *Last Friday Night (T.G.I.F.)*, and *Peacock* all featured, at least in part. The real attraction was backstage interviews with costumers, makeup artists, assistants, and friends, including actress Shannon Woodward. Also interviewed were Katy's sister, Angela, who traveled with the entourage, and her mother and father who insisted they were supportive of their daughter and her career despite conflicts with their views.

The movie was up against *The Amazing Spider-Man* which, not surprisingly, was the winner at the box office. But reviews were positive: Neil Smith of *Total Film* stated, "Despite being as garish and manufactured as Perry's multi-colored hair-don'ts, *Part Of Me* deserves kudos for allowing an element of unpredictability to intrude upon its tween exploitation and sugary vulgarity," while Elizabeth Weitzman of the *New York Daily News* remarked, "Perry may be the world's most high-profile tease, but she sure knows how to show us a good time." As an afterthought, the movie was released on DVD later in the year, turning up in many fans' Christmas stockings.

The movie played a big part in promoting Katy's record releases. One was a new song, *Wide Awake*, which became her next single in summer 2012. It only took two days to record, but wasn't completed in time to make the movie soundtrack. It was her eighth consecutive single to reach the Top 5 of the *Billboard* chart and sold over a million downloads in the States alone, yet "only" made No. 4.

But Katy could afford to smile

at this "failure." She is the only artist ever to spend over 52 consecutive weeks in the Top 10 of the *Billboard* Hot 100, had been nominated for eight Grammy Awards by the end of 2012, and was named 2011's Artist of the Year by MTV. If that eighth US No. 1 single remained in the future, there's no doubt Katy would reach this goal just as she had all the others she'd set herself.

After all the headlines the "Katy and Russell circus" had provided them, the gossip columns waited with bated breath to see who the next love interest in Ms. Perry's life would be. The first man up was Florence + the Machine's guitarist Robert Ackroyd, with whom she was seen holding hands in both Los Angeles and London in the spring of 2012. Surely after being once bitten she wouldn't go for a Brit a second time?

There were rumors Robert would be making California his home to be with her, after the pair were first spotted getting up close and personal at the Coachella Festival in April. But Katy flatly denied a second transatlantic romance was blooming. "There are times I go out and meet people and flirt, but it's not really appropriate to have anything serious." Another man mentioned as the possible next "Mr. Perry" by the ever-probing press was French model Baptiste Giabiconi, the male "face" of Chanel, Fendi, and Karl Lagerfeld.

Then, in the summer, Katy was spotted on a number of occasions with singer-guitarist John Mayer. According to the *Los Angeles Times*, the pair appeared more like a couple with each public outing. They started with a pizza date, then were apparently

holed up writing songs together – probably one of the more intimate things they could have been doing, rather than debating the merits of salami over mozzarella.

Mayer had a list of former girlfriends that, one commentator remarked, amounted to "half the women in Hollywood" and included (deep breath) Taylor Swift, Jennifer Aniston, Jessica Simpson, Minka Kelly, and Jennifer Love Hewitt. It suggested that Katy was setting herself up for more heartbreak. And, indeed, the couple decided to call it quits after a little over two months. *US Magazine* reported Katy was "very upset" with the outcome... but, no doubt realizing she now had to keep certain parts of her life to herself, the 27-year-old singer's tweets said more about her recent conversion to home cooking than the current state of her love life.

For Katy Perry, 2012 had been a great year on the professional front. She'd been on a sold-out worldwide concert tour, released a hit movie, and broken chart records. Sadly, after her divorce she had been facing life mostly on her own. *Billboard* magazine offered a silver lining when, in November, it honored her with its Woman of the Year award.

The singer's strength and resilience in not letting her personal problems affect her work life was certainly to be admired. It was now a question of what the coming year would bring, not least her first album without the guiding hand of Dr. Luke.

The new release would be important in determining if she had Madonna-like longevity. Or would she be a two-album phenomenon who made an impact and would eventually be forgotten when the "next big thing" came along? The next two years would tell if she's going to be a force in music for the next 20. Battling Lady Gaga and Rihanna with every outfit is a phase that surely can't last forever. It might be time to get serious...

With kids, couples, and over 40s in her audience, Katy's appeal was wide-ranging. Her songs seemed to speak to fans of any age and, even those too young to appreciate all the lyrical nuances could happily sing along. If marketing her music to a big audience was a science, she seemed to have it figured out.

But she would surely still want to make a living when she was too old to wear bikinis, polka dots, and brightly-colored wigs, and it was already clear that she found the prospect of a Justin Timberlake-style transition to the movies an attractive one. As one critic put it, "She has ambition and is clever. What she's doing now she won't be doing when she's in her forties. Her music can develop greater depths. She could write for other people and become a brand."

The Madonna comparison was ever-present – no one thought she would still be hitting the headlines at 55, three decades after she burst onto the scene. But Katy has long been a trendsetter through both her music and her style. "My sister never understood the clothes I brought home from vintage stores, and then two years later they were selling the same look at Urban Outfitters."

In July, during a trip to London, Katy told a radio station that her next release would be "darker" than *Teenage Dream*, saying, "I would love to just let it be the 'black box' of who I am." She had previously revealed that she hoped to make an album full of edgy tracks, telling *Interview* magazine, "I think it's time for more meat and potatoes, I feel I have a lot to say.

"With *Teenage Dream*," she continued, "I created this cotton candy cloud with a kind of a wink and a kiss, and it was all cute and fun and playful. (Now) it's like I'm falling from cloud nine and crashing from the sky, crashing from the sweetness of that moment." Yet despite the breakdown of her marriage, she insisted that her new album would not be divorce-themed, telling the UK *Sun* newspaper: "I'd never devote a whole record to heartbreak." She added: "I'm happy, I'm in a good place, I'm looking forward to my future."

One thing was for certain – with fame and fortune now at her fingertips, Katy Perry would be living that future very firmly in the public eye.

CHAPTER 6:
Video Magic

Television had played a major role in the rise of Katy Perry. Her clever, sassy videos had made her an MTV icon. Indeed, she was nominated for no fewer than 10 awards at the channel's 2011 Video Music Awards in August 2011, winning three. (Even in 2012, a relatively quiet year release-wise, she found herself in the running for artist of the year.)

Her visual charm appealed to every age group, from eight to 80. While Lady Gaga went for controversy, Katy was an unthreatening combination of Japanese cartoon and boys' pin-up. Her self-confidence helped her use her looks to promote her music, and that came through in the videos.

After a deliberately low-budget start with *Ur So Gay*, in which Katy performed in front of a backdrop of bright cartoon clouds, with characters played by dolls, the Perry video machine hit its stride with *I Kissed A Girl*. There were many possibilities offered by such a unique song and lyric, and the video, directed by Polish-Australian music video director Kinga Burza, was nominated in two categories for an MTV VMA award.

The clip, which started with Katy lying on a bed unthreateningly stroking a cat and moved on to feature dancers dressed in burlesque costume, let the lyrics stir the controversy as, despite the song's title, there was absolutely no depiction of any kind of same-sex kissing.

The video for *Hot N Cold* saw Katy return to the familiar location of church – this time as a blushing bride about to get hitched to a reluctant groom played by actor/model Alexander Rodriguez. But he escapes and she pursues

him, with her backup dancers/ bridesmaids close behind. This gave her the chance to make multiple costume changes as she sings the song's verses to him in different moods.

The video magic really started with the *California Gurls* video in which Katy first showed off that bikini body – and who can ever forget the bra that squirts whipped cream? "It's definitely something to watch when you have the munchies..." said Katy of the sweetie concept. "It's all edible. We named it 'Candyfornia' instead of 'California' so it's a different world," she said. "It's not just like, 'Oh, let's go to the beach and throw a party and then shoot a music video!' It's more like,

■ **LEFT:** **Katy on the red carpet with children dressed as characters from her music videos.**

'Lets put us California Gurls in a whole different world!'"

Her clip for *Firework* won the MTV Video of the Year award for 2011 – even though it was technically made in 2010. The video was made with European telecommunications group Deutsche Telekom, who recruited Katy Perry fans as its co-stars. A reported 38,000 applicants from all around Europe asked to take part.

The video opened with Katy

C MUSIC MUSIC MUSIC
RDS A

gazing down on the city of Budapest from a castle balcony. As she sang, fireworks shooting from her body light up the sky, inspiring young people to overcome their fears and inhibitions – standing up to bullies and the like. Soon they can be seen flocking to Buda Castle, lighting up the night with their fireworks, and uniting with the singer whose call to arms had lit the touch paper.

It was an amazing clip for a song Katy clearly rated highly. "*California Gurls* is fun and nostalgic," she's said, "but I feel that *Firework* is doing something right because people are affected by it in their own personal way. I'm really proud of it, so I'm really proud the Grammys have nominated that song."

The complexity and cleverness of Katy's videos hit a peak when she turned the clip for *Last Friday Night (T.G.I.F.)* into a mini movie. In an attempt to feed her fans' curiosity, she even took to social media before release as a 13-year-old high-schooler Kathy Beth Terry, who held a house party when her parents were away and got as trashed as the house itself.

The character she played, based on America Ferrera's depiction of Ugly Betty, underwent a Cinderella-like transformation to take the floor in fluorescent pink top and green skirt. Guests in the video included saxophonist Kenny G, *Glee* stars Daren Kriss (Blaine) and Kevin McHale (Artie), YouTube singing discovery Rebecca Black, and Nineties pop group Hanson. *Lost Boys* actor Corey Feldman and Eighties pop starlet Debbie Gibson played her parents in the video, which was directed by Marc Klasfeld.

But even that was surpassed by *The One That Got Away*, in which Katy played an older version of herself looking back to a former boyfriend who died in an auto crash after they had argued. Now trapped in a loveless marriage, she went back in time to meet her younger self and to try and make peace with her lost lover.

An entranced Jocelyn Vena of MTV News said: "Perry's moody, contemplative clip for *The One That Got Away* perfectly encapsulates both the joy of falling in love and the heartbreak of letting go. It travels through time and space and recalls the story of Perry's one that got away."

Shooting videos has been great training for the Hollywood-bound Katy. But it's also been hard work. "What I really found out was that acting is very hard. It's not that easy. Doing a music video is very different than doing a movie. A video is five or six days going 13 to 15 hours a day, and that's a lot for me. It takes a lot of discipline and self-control."

It's clear from this and the other video clips she's been responsible for that Katy Perry ultimately sees her future on the big screen. Her talents and endless ideas appear to make her a natural – we can only hope that she doesn't turn her back on the music world in favor of a full-time Hollywood career.

Discography

Singles

Ur So Gay
Released November 2007
US chart position –

I Kissed A Girl
Released April 2008
US chart position 1

Hot N Cold
Released September 2008
US chart position 3

Thinking Of You
Released January 2009
US chart position 29

Waking Up In Vegas
Released April 2009
US chart position 9

California Gurls
Released May 2010
US chart position 1

Teenage Dream
Released July 2010
US chart position 1

Firework
Released October 2010
US chart position 1

E.T.
Released February 2011
US chart position 1

Last Friday Night (T.G.I.F.)
Released June 2011
US chart position 1

The One That Got Away
Released October 2011
US chart position 3

Part Of Me
Released February 2012
US chart position 1

Wide Awake
Released May 2012
US chart position 4

Albums

Katy Hudson
Released October 2001
US chart position –
Trust In Me – Piercing – Search Me – Last Call – Growing Pains – My Own Monster – Spit – Faith Won't Fail – Naturally – When There's Nothing Left

One Of The Boys
Released June 2008
US chart position 9
One Of The Boys – I Kissed A Girl – Waking Up In Vegas – Thinking Of You – Mannequin – Ur So Gay – Hot N Cold – If You Can Afford Me – Lost – Self Inflicted – I'm Still Breathing – Fingerprints

MTV Unplugged
Released November 2009
US chart position 168
I Kissed A Girl – Ur So Gay – Hackensack – Thinking Of You – Lost – Waking Up In Vegas – Brick By Brick
Also released as a DVD.

Teenage Dream
Released August 2010
US chart position 1
Teenage Dream – Last Friday Night (T.G.I.F.) – California Gurls – Firework – Peacock – Circle The Drain – The One That Got Away – E.T. – Who Am I Living For? – Pearl – Hummingbird – Heartbeat – Not Like The Movies

Last Word: Perry's Pals

■ **ABOVE:** Kelly Clarkson.

You've got to have friends in the music business, as in any walk of life – and Katy Perry has plenty! Of course we all know that Snoop Dogg turned up in the video clip for *California Gurls*, but did you know Katy guested on a single, *If We Ever Meet Again*, by fellow rapper Timbaland, in 2009? Another rap connection came when Perry released a *The One That Got Away* remix featuring B.o.B in late 2011.

Likewise, Katy's work as vocalist with The Matrix is well known. But in 2009 she joined forces with electronic rock group 3OH!3 on the single *Starstrukk*. It failed to rise higher than No. 66 in the States but hit the Top 5 in the United Kingdom, Belgium, and Australia.

Katy is prolific as a songwriter and, as of 2012, had written songs for other singers, including Selena Gomez & the Scene (*Rock God* and *That's More Like It*), Kelly Clarkson (*Long Shot* and the previously mentioned *I Do Not Hook Up*), Ashley Tisdale (*Time's Up*), Jessie James (*Bullet* and *Girl Next Door*), Lesley Roy (*Slow Goodbye*), and Kady Malloy (*Wish You The Worst*). More will undoubtedly follow.

It's this ability to willingly collaborate and share the spotlight that point to a long career in the music business for Katheryn Elizabeth Hudson, aka Katy Perry. And since it's her long-held ambition to own a record label, who's to say she won't be guiding the careers of a new generation of pop starlets in 20 years' time? We'd put money on it!

■ **ABOVE: Selena Gomez attends the premiere of *Katy Perry: Part Of Me*.**

■ **RIGHT: Jessie James.**

Katy in Quotes

"I got this Jesus tattoo on my wrist when I was 18 because I know that it's always going to be a part of me. When I'm playing, it's staring right back at me, saying, 'Remember where you came from.'"

"I'm a good flirt. I'll buy a person a drink, and then catch him off guard, before he can even open his mouth. I like to take the upper hand a little bit and then see if he can bring me down to size."

"*Peacock* is a whole other side to my personality, that's like more messed up, silly, sarcastic, and full of irony. I'm really such a heavy lyricist in all my music, like I really try and give words a different dimension and make them double entendres and hidden innuendos."

"I like to kiss boys, but there is no doubt in my mind if Angelina Jolie or Gisele Bündchen came a callin', who wouldn't pucker up?"

"The records are black boxes for me. If you want to know who I am, my views, my perspective, things I love, things I hate, my convictions, my anthems... I've never let people's opinions affect the way I write."

"It's important to be relatable and normal. And I think that what helps with that, for me, is that I had the rug pulled out from underneath my feet so many times. It was like, 'Listen up, you're not going to get served this on a silver platter, you've got to work for it!' I still have so much to prove."

"I'm on this extraordinary adventure, and if I have no one to talk to at the end of the night I feel lonely."

"There is an obvious element in me that wants to entertain people and make their faces light up."

"I think that, whenever anyone writes something that is different than, like, your plain peanut butter and jelly song, 'I love you, you love me,' everyone kind of perks up and says, 'What's *this*?'"

"I don't feel like I'm very pop-star lame, but I'm definitely not hipster-cool. I'm somewhere right in the middle of it all. Because, for me, I want to sell out, but just not in the 'I've sold out' kind of way. I want to sell out arenas and sell millions of records."

"I don't follow trends. I'm just not into what everyone else is wearing. I have my own look, which I call 'Lolita Meets Old Hollywood Glam.' But there are certain times when I want to mix it up and be edgier."